You can Save the Planet

Something Old, Something New: Recycling

Anita Ganeri

www.heinemann.co.uk/library
Visit our website to find out more information about Heinemann Library books.

To order:
☎ Phone 44 (0) 1865 888066
🖹 Send a fax to 44 (0) 1865 314091
🖳 Visit the Heinemann Bookshop at www.heinemann.co.uk/library to browse our catalogue and order online.

First published in Great Britain by Heinemann Library, Halley Court, Jordan Hill, Oxford OX2 8EJ, part of Harcourt Education. Heinemann is a registered trademark of Harcourt Education Ltd.

Editorial: Nancy Dickmann and Dave Harris
Design: Richard Parker and Q2A Solutions
Illustrations: Q2A
Picture Research: Maria Joannou and Virginia Stroud-Lewis
Production: Camilla Smith

Originated by Dot Gradations Limited
Printed in China by WKT Company Limited

ISBN 0 431 04168 7
09 08 07 06 05
10 9 8 7 6 5 4 3 2 1

British Library Cataloguing in Publication Data
Ganeri, Anita
Something Old, Something New: Recycling.
– (You Can Save the Planet)
363.7'282
A full catalogue record for this book is available from the British Library.

Acknowledgements
The publishers would like to thank the following for permission to reproduce photographs: Alamy pp. **9**, **14**, **16**; Corbis/Jean Heguy p. **15**; Corbis/Lester Lefkowitz p. **12**; Corbis/Michael S. Yamashita p. **20**; Ecoscene p. **24**; Getty Images/Image Bank p. **13**; ICCE/Mark Boulton p. **5**; Panos Pictures/Chris Sattlberger p. **26**; Panos Pictures/Tim Dirven p. **23**; Photofusion/Dorothy Burrows p. **27**; Science Photo Library/Simon Fraser/Northumbrian Environmental Management Ltd. p. **8**; Tudor Photography pp. **4**, **7**, **10**, **11**, **17**, **18**, **19**, **21**, **22**, **25**.

Cover photograph of a girl recycling drink cans, reproduced with permission of Ecoscene/Angela Hampton.

The publishers would like to thank Nick Lapthorn of the Field Studies Council for his assistance in the preparation of this book.

Every effort has been made to contact copyright holders of any material reproduced in this book. Any omissions will be rectified in subsequent printings if notice is given to the publishers.

The paper used to print this book comes from sustainable resources.

contents

Words appearing in the text in bold, **like this**, are explained in the Glossary.

What is waste?

Waste is anything we throw away. We throw away some things, such as drink cans and newspapers, because we do not need them any more. We throw away other things, such as toys and fridges, when they are broken or worn out.

What is the problem?

Waste is a big problem for our planet. We have to find places to put all the waste we throw away, and we are running out of space. Besides, every time we throw something away, we waste precious materials. Waste is bad for the **environment**. It can harm and kill plants and animals, including humans.

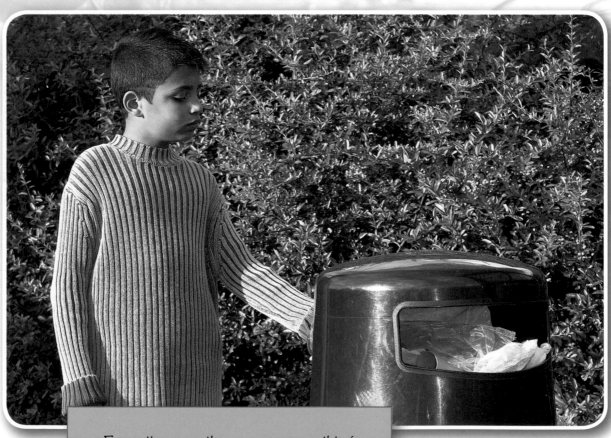

Every time you throw away something, you are wasting the material in it and the energy used to make it.

The three Rs

We need to find ways to throw less waste away. There are three ways to do this. These are known as the three Rs. The first R is for reduce, which means cutting down on the things we buy so that we have to throw less away. The second R is for reuse, which means using old things again instead of throwing them away. The third R is for recycle, which means making new things out of old. Things should only be thrown away when we cannot reuse or recycle them.

These are shoes made from reused car tyres.

Taking Action: What can I do?

If we keep throwing away so much waste, we are storing up problems for people in the future. You might think that the problem of waste is too big for you to do anything about. But if each of us makes a small effort, together we can make a big difference. Look out for Taking Action boxes like this one throughout this book. They will give you ideas for things you can do to reduce, reuse, and recycle.

What do we throw away?

Think about all the waste you made today. You might be surprised. Among the things you might have thrown away are cereal packets, plastic milk bottles, used writing paper, drink cans, snack wrappers, and apple cores. But you are not alone. The rest of your family makes waste, too. So does every other family, office, shop, school, and factory in your town and country. That is an enormous amount of waste.

How much waste?

In **developed** countries, such as the UK, the USA, and Australia, each household throws away about a tonne of waste every year. Each year we throw away more waste than the year before. In most developed countries, only about a tenth of this waste is reused or recycled. This chart shows how much and what sort of waste a typical household in a developed country throws away.

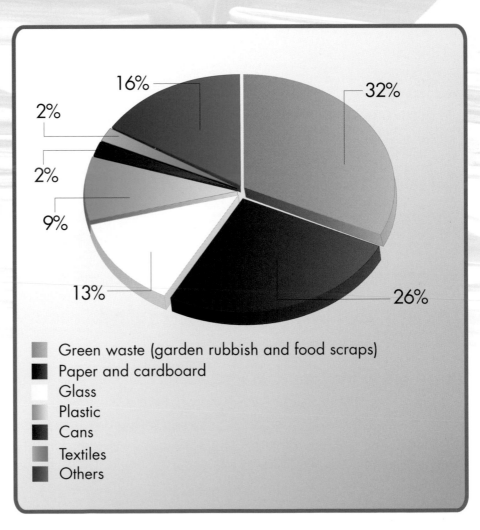

16%
32%
2%
2%
9%
13%
26%

- Green waste (garden rubbish and food scraps)
- Paper and cardboard
- Glass
- Plastic
- Cans
- Textiles
- Others

Every day we throw away many types of materials. Some could be recycled.

Wasted energy

It takes lots of energy to make brand-new things. For example, the energy used to make an aluminium drinks can in a factory would power a television for three hours. When we throw something away, we are also throwing away the energy used to make it. Energy is precious. Most of it comes from burning **fossil fuels**, which harms the environment.

Taking Action: A waste diary

Try keeping a waste diary for a week at home or school. Ask a parent or teacher to help. At the end of each day, empty all the bins at home or in your classroom into one bag and weigh it. Draw a chart that shows the weight of waste you collect each day. Work out the weekly waste total.

Where does our waste go?

Waste is collected from your home or school by waste trucks. Machinery in the trucks crushes the waste so that it takes up less space. The trucks unload the waste at a **waste transfer station**. Some waste is taken away to be recycled. Some waste is burned. The rest is taken to places called **landfill** sites.

Dozens of trucks dump their loads of rubbish into a landfill site every day.

What happens at a landfill site?

At a landfill site, waste is tipped into a huge hole. The hole is lined with plastic and clay to keep liquid from the waste from leaking out. When the site is full, the waste is covered with a layer of soil. But we should not forget about the buried waste. Dangerous liquids and gases can come from the site, and some of the waste will take thousands of years to **rot** away. Landfill sites also look ugly and smell bad. After a few years, parks or golf courses can be built on the site. But it is hard to build houses because the ground sinks as the waste rots.

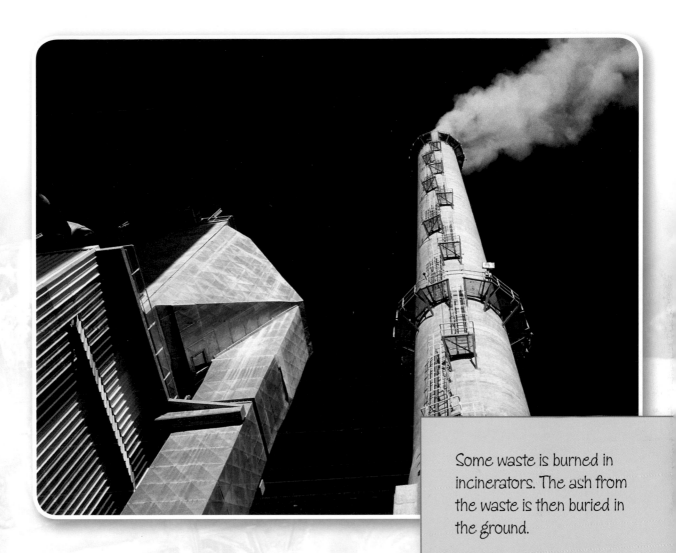

Some waste is burned in incinerators. The ash from the waste is then buried in the ground.

Science Behind It: Liquid and gas

Some waste rots away naturally in landfill sites, just as dead plants rot away in the garden. But as the waste rots, it makes **methane** gas, which is explosive. Rotting also makes a black liquid called leachate, which can contain dangerous chemicals. Both the methane and leachate can be dangerous if they leak into the ground around the site. They must be collected for many years after the site is full.

What are the three Rs?

What is reducing?

Reducing is the first of the three Rs. It means not buying things that will be thrown away soon after buying them. Reducing is the best way of cutting down waste. Next time you go shopping, try to think how you can reduce the amount you buy and so reduce the amount you waste.

Taking Action

Here are some ideas for reducing waste:

- Try not to buy things with lots of **packaging**. You will just throw it away when you get home. For example, buy loose apples instead of apples packed on a tray and covered with plastic.
- Take your lunch and snacks to school in reusable plastic containers instead of wrapping them in foil or plastic food wrap.
- Reuse scraps of coloured paper and **textiles** as art materials at school.
- Don't buy **disposable** things. For example, if you are going on a picnic, don't buy paper plates and plastic knifes and forks which you will later throw away. Take proper plates and metal cutlery instead.
- Buy good quality things that will last a long time.
- Use **rechargeable batteries** instead of disposable batteries.

Some things we buy have more packaging than they need. How much waste does this create?

What is reusing?

Reusing is the second of the three Rs. Reusing means using things again, instead of throwing them away. Some things can be used again in the same way. For example, you can reuse envelopes several times before they are worn out. You can also reuse things in a new way. For example, you could use an old plastic margarine tub for storing paper clips.

Make your desk tidy with reused food containers.

Taking Action: Sell and donate

Try not to throw anything away that somebody else could use. This might be old toys and games, videos, books, ornaments, and clothes that your family does not want any more. Instead, collect them up and organize a sale with your friends. You could hold the sale at school, in your garage or at a car boot sale. You could also give the things to a local charity shop.

What is recycling?

Recycling is the third of the three Rs. Recycling means using the materials in old objects to make new objects. For example, the glass in old bottles can be recycled to make new bottles. The aluminium in old drink cans can be used to make new cans. Some materials can be recycled hundreds of times.

These trees have been cut down to make things for people to use, such as paper.

Why should we recycle?

There are two main reasons for recycling. It saves the precious **natural resources** needed to make new materials. For example, when you recycle paper, fewer trees need to be cut down to make new paper. When you recycle plastic, oil and natural gas supplies do not have to be used to make new plastic. Recycling also saves energy and other resources such as water and chemicals. Recycling is not always the best thing to do. Some materials use more energy to recycle than to make new.

What can we recycle?

Hundreds of different things can be recycled, from plastic bottles to whole cars. It is easiest to recycle things that are made of just one material, such as newspapers, glass bottles, or aluminium cans. These things are broken down or melted. More complicated things, such as computers and fridges, have to be taken apart to separate out the different materials.

Science Behind It: Does recycling save energy?

Making anything uses energy. Think of a food can made of steel. It took energy to mine the rock that the iron came from. Then the rock has to be transported to the metal works where the iron is taken out of the rock, made into steel, and made into the can. By recycling the can, almost all of that energy can be saved.

The materials used to make steel cans must be heated to a very high temperature. This uses lots of energy.

collecting for recycling

Your house and school might have special recycling bins where you collect paper, glass, plastic, or a mixture of different materials. You probably also have a local recycling centre where you can take things that cannot go in the bin, such as textiles, batteries, and appliances such as fridges.

This logo tells you that something can be recycled, or that it is made from recycled materials.

Always sort waste properly before putting it into recycling bins.

Taking your waste for recycling is a very good idea. But do not make a special trip in a car to your recycling centre if you have only got one or two bottles or newspapers to throw away. The **pollution** from the car and the energy used up would cancel out all the good you would be doing by recycling!

Taking Action: Buy recycled

It is only worth companies making things from recycled materials if people are happy to buy them. So the best way to encourage recycling is to buy recycled things when you can. Look out for the recycled logo on things such as waste sacks, toilet paper and paper towels. At school, find out if writing paper and toilet paper are made from recycled paper.

Can we cut down on waste paper?

Every day, we throw away millions of newspapers and magazines, huge piles of printing paper, envelopes, junk mail, and cardboard. Paper and cardboard make up about quarter of all **household waste**. Offices throw even more away. By putting the three Rs into action, you can easily cut down on how much paper you waste.

This is a large pile of old newspapers and magazines. Think of the trees that were cut down to make them!

Reducing and reusing paper

There are lots of ways of cutting down on the amount of paper and cardboard you use at school and at home. Here are some ideas:

- Always write on both sides of a sheet of paper.
- Don't start a new page in a notebook until the last page is finished.
- Only print out what you really need when using a computer.
- Share newspapers and magazines with your friends instead of buying one each.
- Reuse cardboard boxes for storage.
- Ask your family to cancel junk mail, if they can.

Taking Action: Paper recycling

Paper is one of the easiest materials to recycle. You can buy recycled writing paper and wrapping paper. Many newspapers are printed on recycled paper. At home, make sure newspapers, magazines, and other types of paper are recycled if possible. Do you have a paper recycling scheme at school? If not, ask your teachers if you can start one. Arrange for your classmates to put waste paper in a separate bin. Advertise your scheme by putting up posters and on your school website.

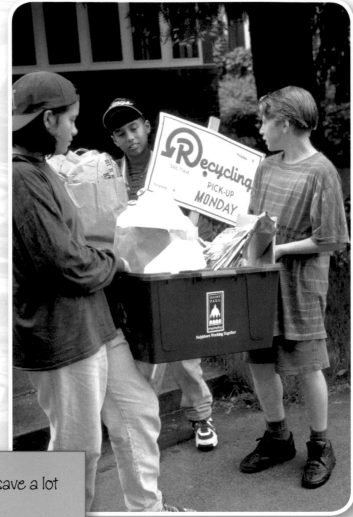

A few seconds spent recycling can save a lot of energy and a lot of trees!

Science Behind It: New and recycled paper

Paper is made from tiny **fibres** glued together. Most of the fibres come from conifer trees that have been specially grown for making paper. The wood is mashed and broken up to get the fibres out. Turning trees into paper uses lots of energy, water, and other chemicals. Recycling paper saves trees and energy.

Case Study: Paper for worms

When the children at Mildura West Primary School in Australia looked into recycling, they found that some types of paper, such as envelopes and used photocopier paper, could not be recycled in their area. Instead, it went into **landfill** sites. The children discovered a clever way of reusing the paper. Worms can eat shredded paper, so the children decided to shred their waste paper and send it to local worm farms, where worms are grown for fishermen to use as bait.

The children put up posters to advertise their scheme to local people and invited experts to talk to pupils and parents. They told local people how to collect and shred waste paper and organised a scheme to collect the paper from people's homes. The school was given money to buy two paper-shredding machines. In 2003, the school won a Waste Wise award for their work.

One good way to reuse paper is to feed it to worms. The worms can then be sold.

Can we recycle old Cans?

The answer is: yes, we can! Most drink cans are made from aluminium. Most food cans are made from steel. You can recycle both of these metals. Collect your cans in a box. Ask your **local authority** where you can take them to be recycled. As well as saving **natural resources**, you will also be saving energy. It takes twenty times more energy to make a new aluminium drink can than to make one from recycled metal.

What about other metal things?

Most metal things can be recycled. Like drink cans, kitchen foil and foil food dishes are made from aluminium. Collect a box full and take them for recycling. You can also take larger metal objects, such as old bicycle frames, to your recycling centre.

If a magnet sticks to the can, it is probably made of steel. If it does not stick, it is probably made of aluminium. Steel and aluminium cans are often recycled separately.

Science Behind It: Metals from rocks

Metals such as aluminium are **extracted** from rocks called ores. First, the ore is dug from the ground and crushed. Then, it is heated in a container until it melts. This releases the aluminium. Electricity is passed through the molten (melted) ore, which makes the aluminium flow out. The aluminium cools and turns to solid metal. All this uses a lot of energy, which is why it is better to recycle metals.

Can we use glass again?

Glass makes up about five to ten per cent of **household waste**. If you live in a **developed** country, your family could throw away as many as 500 glass jars and bottles every year. Unfortunately, glass does not **rot** away. It lasts for thousands of years in a **landfill** site. All of this waste glass could be reused or recycled.

How can we reuse glass?

You can use some glass bottles and jars again and again. For example, empty glass jars make vases for flowers or can be used for storing small objects such as pens and paper clips. Glass jars also make excellent pots for mixing and storing paints. Sometimes glass is crushed into small chunks and mixed to make road surfaces.

You can reuse glass jars by keeping things in them instead of throwing them away.

Science Behind It: Recycling bottles

Glass is made from sand, a material called soda ash, and limestone. These ingredients are melted together and poured into moulds to make bottles. By recycling glass, we save digging up and using these **raw materials**. Glass bottles are easy to recycle. They are crushed to make a material called cullet, which is melted down and then used to make new bottles.

This shows uncrushed glass bottles on the right and crushed glass cullet on the left at a a recycling centre.

Taking Action: Sorting glass

Glass comes in different colours. The main colours are clear, brown, and green. If these colours are mixed when they are recycled, the new glass comes out looking muddy. So glass bottles and jars must be sorted into these colours before they are recycled. When you take glass bottles to your recycling centre, make sure you put them in the correct bins. Glass from household recycling bins is sorted when it arrives at the glass recycling centre. Always be very careful when you handle glass in case it is broken.

What can we do with old plastic?

Plastic is a very useful material. It can be moulded into almost any shape. We use it to make thousands of objects, from tiny toys to garden furniture. Every year, we throw away millions of plastic bags, bottles, and containers. Unfortunately, plastic does not **rot** away. It lasts for hundreds of years. Plastic is made from oil and natural gas. Wasting plastic also wastes these precious supplies. Oil and natural gas supplies will not last forever, and when they run out there will be no more.

Many of the things we buy and use every day are packaged in plastic. Most of the plastic gets thrown away, but some could be recycled.

The simplest way to cut down the amount of plastic we throw away is to reduce the plastic **packaging** we buy. You can help by not buying things that have lots of plastic packaging around them. You can also reuse plastic containers. For example, ice-cream tubs make excellent storage containers, and you can refill plastic bottles with drinks to take to school.

Can plastic be recycled?

There are more than fifty different types of plastic. Some plastics cannot be recycled. Some can be recycled but cannot be mixed together. This means we have to sort plastics carefully before they can be recycled. Plastics that can be recycled usually have a symbol on them. However, there may not be facilities to recycle all plastics in your area. Always wash out plastic bottles and containers before you recycle them.

Recycled plastics are used to make hundreds of different objects, such as bin liners, carrier bags, and other packaging, as well as drain pipes and signposts. Some fleece jackets are made from recycled fizzy drinks bottles.

Carefully check the symbols on your plastic bottles, to see which types of plastic they are.

Taking Action: Plastic bags for life

In the UK, people throw away about 8 billion plastic bags every year, and Australians throw away about 6 billion! You can easily reuse plastic bags by taking them back to the shop the next time you visit. Or you can use them for kitchen waste instead of buying bin bags. Better still, buy a strong shopping bag that will last for hundreds of shopping trips.

Case Study: Reusing spectacles

Most spectacle lenses are made from plastic. They are expensive to make because the plastic must be very pure and the lenses must be made very accurately. They cannot be made from recycled plastic. Spectacle frames are also expensive to make. Spectacles are not usually recycled because they do not contain enough plastic and metal to make it worthwhile. Millions of pairs of spectacles are thrown away every year. However, a charity called Vision Aid Overseas has found a way to reuse spectacles and to help poor people at the same time.

How are spectacles reused?

In many countries, people with poor eyesight cannot afford spectacles, and life is difficult for them. Vision Aid Overseas collects old spectacles in Britain. Then **opticians** take them to poorer countries such as Kenya and India. The opticians test people's eyesight and give them the right spectacles to wear.

This girl will be able to see better with the reused spectacles she is being given.

Can we recycle plants?

About a quarter of **household waste** is plant waste from kitchens and gardens. It is mostly made of fruit and vegetable peelings, grass cuttings, and weeds. This can be called 'green waste'. Green waste **rots** naturally, but it causes problems when it is buried in **landfill** sites. It takes up lots of space, and it produces **methane** gas. But you can easily recycle green waste at school and at home to make **compost**.

Can we use methane?

Methane can be useful. At some landfill sites, methane is collected and sent to nearby factories, where it is burned for heating. This methane is called biogas. Plant waste can be put into special containers called digesters. Here it rots to produce methane, which can be burned for heating and cooking.

This small-scale biogas system was designed to heat the house.

Science Behind It: What is biodegradable?

Dead plants and animals are biodegradable. This means that they rot away naturally. They rot because **micro-organisms** such as **bacteria** and **fungi** feed on them. The micro-organisms turn the remains into simple chemicals that mix into the soil, where new plants use them to grow. In this way, dead plants and animals are recycled naturally. Materials such as metals, glass, and plastic are not biodegradable.

Taking Action: Making compost

Compost is easy to make. You can buy a compost bin or make one from scrap wood. Put the bin on a patch of soil in a sunny place. Simply put green waste into the bin and mix it with a fork. After about six months, the compost at the bottom of the bin will have turned dark and crumbly. Now it is ready to put on the garden. You can compost:

- vegetable and fruit peelings
- grass cuttings
- hedge trimmings
- leaves
- used tea bags and coffee beans
- shredded paper.

You should not put any meat, fish scraps, or cooked food into compost. It will attract mice and other pests.

Adding a good mixture of different vegetable wastes to your compost bin makes good, rich compost.

What else can we recycle?

There are not many things that cannot be reused or recycled. To reuse old clothes, put them in a **textile** recycling bin or give them to a charity shop. Furniture can also be reused. Even complicated machines can be broken up and their parts recycled. But you should first try to mend a machine if it goes wrong, before throwing it away and buying a new one.

What happens to old computers?

Old computers are difficult to sell because they are too slow and do not have enough memory to use the latest software. However, there are organizations that take old computers and **refurbish** them. They erase the hard discs, add more memory, and put in faster processors. Then the computers can be used for jobs where the most powerful computers are not necessary, such as word-processing. Some refurbished computers are donated to people who cannot afford new machines.

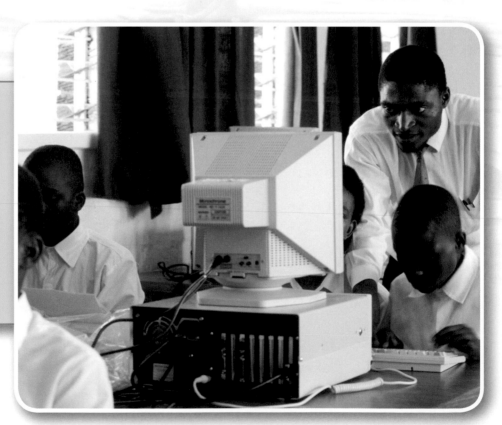

This is a computer class in a school in Zimbabwe. The children are using refurbished computers that were donated by a charity.

What other machines can we recycle?

Fridges, washing machines, dishwashers, and cookers take up lots of space in **landfill** sites. Instead, they can be broken up and their parts recycled. Many car parts can also be recycled. Old parts, such as oil and batteries, can be recycled. Tyres can be reused to make crash barriers, chopped up to make soft playground surfaces, and even cut up to make soles for shoes. Modern cars are designed so that many parts are easy to remove for recycling after the car is worn out.

Taking Action: Collect for charity

Charities often collect old mobile phones and computer printer cartridges, which they recycle to raise money. Why not organize a collection of old mobile phones and ink cartridges at your school? Look on the Internet to find out which charities you can donate them to. Make a collection bin and a poster to advertise what you are doing.

This is a recycling bank which collects printer cartridges and mobile phones. Find out if there is one near where you live!

Fact file

- In a year, the 60 million inhabitants of the UK produce about 500 million tonnes of waste. This would fill a line of trucks that would stretch five times around the world.
- Each year, we produce about 3% more waste than the year before. If we take no action, the amount of waste we make will double by the year 2020.
- Each American citizen creates 2 kilograms (4.5 pounds) of **household waste** every day. Together, Americans produce about 210 million tonnes of household waste.
- Each year Americans throw away enough cardboard to fill 5000 Olympic-sized swimming pools.
- Seven out of every ten newspapers are recycled in Australia. This saves over a billion newspapers from going to waste!
- Every year a typical household in the UK throws away:
    - 500 glass bottles and jars
    - 1000 food and drink cans
    - 400 plastic bags
    - Ten truck loads of green waste
    - Six trees worth of paper
- 80 million cans go into **landfill** sites in the UK every day.
- 8 million **disposable** nappies are thrown away in the UK every day.
- Americans throw away 2.5 million plastic bottles every hour!
- Recycling an aluminium can saves enough electricity to run a computer for three hours.

Find out more

Books to read

Awesome Things to Make with Recycled Stuff, Joe Rhatigan and Heather Smith (Sterling Juvenile Books, 2004)

Green Files: Waste and Recycling, Steve Parker (Heinemann Library, 2004)

Websites

There are many useful websites to help you learn more and make plans for taking action of your own.

Waste Watch – promotes reducing, reusing and recycling in the UK:
www.wastewatch.org.uk

Recyclezone – Waste Watch site for children and schools:
www.recyclezone.org.uk

Aluminium Packaging Recycling Organisation – find out about recycling aluminium:
www.alupro.org.uk

Planet Ark – Australian environmental website:
www.planetark.com

Vision Aid Overseas – spectacle recycling charity:
www.vao.org.uk

Computer Aid International – charity which recycles computers:
www.computer-aid.org

Glossary

bacteria tiny living things that live in air, water, or soil

compost material that helps plants grow, which is made from the remains of rotting plants

developed describes a country that has advanced industries and where most people have an education, jobs, a place to live, and food to eat

disposable something that is designed to be thrown away after being used

environment our surroundings, including plants and animals, the land, water, and atmosphere, and buildings

extract remove from something

fibre very thin piece of something

fossil fuel fuel that is formed from the remains of plants and animals that died millions of years ago. Fossil fuels include coal, gas, and oil.

fungi living things such as mushrooms, toadstools and moulds. They are niether plants nor animals.

household waste waste that is made by the people who live in a home

landfill place where waste is buried in deep holes in the ground

local authority government of a particular area

methane gas given off by rotting plants

micro-organism plant, animal or other living thing that is too small to see with the naked eye

natural resource useful material that we get from our natural surroundings, such as wood, coal, and rocks

optician person who tests people's sight and works out what spectacles they need

packaging material used to wrap up things you buy, such as plastic bags and cardboard boxes

pollution something that makes air, water, or other parts of the Earth's environment dirty

raw material material we get from the Earth in its natural state, which we can then use to make other things

rechargeable battery battery that can be used again and again by putting electricity back into it when it has run out

refurbish repair and add new parts to an old machine so that it can be used again

rot break down into simple chemicals naturally

textile material used to make clothing and furnishings

waste transfer station place where people can take their waste to be recycled or taken to landfill sites

Index

Titles in the *You Can Save The Planet* series include:

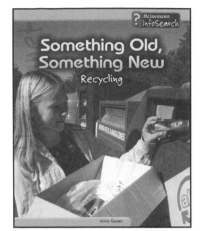

Hardback   0 431 04168 7

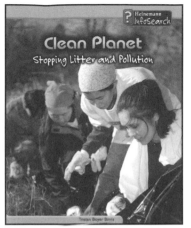

Hardback   0 431 04171 7

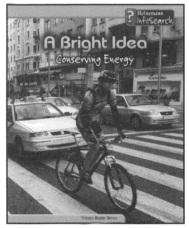

Hardback   0 431 04169 5

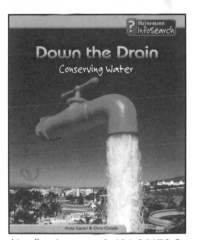

Hardback   0 431 04170 9

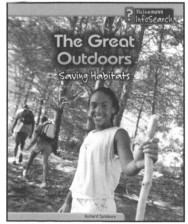

Hardback   0 431 04172 5

Find out about other titles from Heinemann Library on our website www.heinemann.co.uk/library